The Exile

Spanish Notes 1964-2000

Anthony Edkins

Hearing Eye

Published by
Hearing Eye
99 Torriano Avenue, London, NW5 2RX

Copyright © Anthony Edkins, 2001

This publication has been made possible with the financial assistance of London Arts

Printed by Catford Print Centre
3 Bellingham Road
Bellingham, Catford, London SE6 2PN
Tel: 020 8695 0101
Typeset by Daniel James at mondo designo
Cover illustration by Lucy Edkins

ISBN 1 870841 80 8

Acknowledgments

Some of these poems first appeared in Adam, Ambit, Galley Sail Review (USA), Iconolatre, Palantir, Spirit (USA) and West Coast Review (Canada); Notes from Abroad was included in Rock Pool (Hearing Eye, 1992).

Contents

The Exile (1964-1989)

The Exile	6
Midday in Madrid	8
Homage to Giuseppe Fanelli	9
Catalan Painter	10
The Nineteenth of August	11
Things Seen in Spain	12
Conquistador	13
Incident near Montserrat	15
Madrid: An Old Blind Woman	17
Craftsman	18
On Reading César Vallejo at Midnight	19
Notes from Abroad	20
Visit to a Dying Friend	21
Doctor Esquerdo Street, Madrid	21
Welcome to Spain	22
Picasso	23

Patria (1990-2000)

The Bulls of Guisando or the Stillness of Stones	27
Spanish Character	28
Revisiting Luarca: 1991	29
1492: Cowboys and Indians	30
Domenicos Theotocopoulos Becomes El Greco	31
Gredos: 1952	31
Yerma's Spain	32
'For poets'	33
Costa Brava: 1959	33
'There was a young poet of Vigo'	33
Comparative Literature	34
Some Important Revelations about Picasso	35
Charter Flight to Bilbao	36
Religious Sonnet	37
Portuguesswork	38
'There was an Old Master'	38
Chillida's 'Peine del Viento'	39
For Antonio Machado	39
'Goya's Disasters of War'	40
A Stab at Semantics	40
San Juan de Nieves: 1953	41
Castille: 1983	41
The Distance of Spain	42
Patria	43

THE EXILE (1964-1989)

The Exile

González
in his usual wicker chair
chainsmoking Gauloises
gesticulating, garrulous:
the politics of art
the art of politics
the sons of bitches
who cut short their stumbling liberty
and shot or exiled
anyone
who painted, wrote poetry
or wept...

González generalizes
about a Spain he last saw
nearly thirty years ago,
most probably
has never been to Ibiza
Benidorm, Tossa, Torremolinos;
the tourists
(changing trains in Paris)
know these places well
have not heard of Jarama
Brunete, Huesca, Teruel;
Hiroshima
was more spectacular
than Guernica
but González
(who lived through both)
has almost forgotten the former;
the tourists at the next table
tell him about Spanish hoteliers,
he does not understand —

the Spain he knew was a land of poets;
they show him snaps of civil guards
in patent leather hats,
he sees them,
with out-of-focus hate-filled eyes,
not as camera-bait, but as killers...

González lights another Gauloise
starts to speak again:
'Spain—'
someone interrupts:
'—Spain began falling to pieces
centuries ago
when they killed off or kicked out
the Jews and the Moors...'
González leans forward
to warm himself with argument,
trying to re-live
the Madrilenian *tertulias*
of his youth
beneath this colder Parisian sky.

Midday in Madrid

At midday these people
hurrying in pairs or singly
to and from the centre of the city,
are still quite crisp;

there is no shade at noon,
nevertheless, sprayed with water,
the streets, pavements, short grass, flowering shrubs
and trees smell fresh;

two meet, shake hands and nod,
they pat each other on the back,
constrain or guide by holding an elbow,
part unruffled;

on each side of the street
a crowd gathers waiting to cross,
traffic lights change colour, a whistle blows,
they surge, released;

at noon they still hurry,
their energy not yet run down,
geared to the momentum of the city,
alert, active...

but soon the only ones
to move will do so furtively,
to avoid exposure in the silent
afternoon sun.

Homage to Giuseppe Fanelli

Cities are full of statues
commemorating thieves and rogues:
sir something this, the duke of that,
marshal law in a cocked hat;
tyrants in diverse disguises —
saviours upon white horses,
reformers whose deeds drown their words
and liberators with their swords;
sometimes, as a sop to culture,
poets are thrown to the vultures;
here and there, released from dungeons,
a patriot is perch for pigeons;
and, of course, in every city
— monumental hypocrisy! —
an unknown soldier, head bowed down,
guards the dead conscience of the town.

Keep the poets — if their words were
for everyman and everywhere —
but scrap the rest, and in their place
hoist heroes of the human race
who sang the brotherhood of man
and not man's triumph over man.

Fanelli, for example, whose name
is little known, even in Spain
where, as anarchy's apostle
he performed a miracle
of speech: by power of will and lung
he made his Italian tongue
preach freedom to Spaniards;
they could not understand his words
but what he said they understood —
freedom, justice, brotherhood!

Keep the poets — if their words are
for everyman and everywhere —
but scrap the rest and in their place
put heroes of the human race
who sing the brotherhood of man
and not man's triumph over man.

Catalan Painter

Miró is in his element beside the sea
digs castles sifts sand catches driftwood sees starfish
certain shells remind him about seafood
and crustaceous appetites;
visceral shapes diurnal summers
hot hard handsome human handshakes
¿cómo va?
the round red sun falls — *¡pam!*
¡pa-ta-pum!

Tomorrow, prickly hot
the same sharp confusion
among the rocks on the sand
the nursery floor and studio
of Joan Miró
Catalan painter.

The Nineteenth of August

There's one death we shan't ever forgive:
death of a poet in the sun,
poet of red wounds and kisses
kissed by the blackened mouth of a gun;

there's one death we can't ever forgive:
death of a poet in the sun,
poet of white moon and lilies,
lilies and wounds through which the words run;

there are deaths that we'll never forget,
deaths of poets in the daylight,
poets like dark gypsy riders
riding the wild horses of the night;

there are deaths that we'll never forget,
deaths of poets in the daylight,
poets of red blood and water,
water's panic and the wind's dawn flight;

there are deaths we'll always remember
through the dead poet's eyes,

eyes that last saw the black mouth of a gun
shouting down Andalucía's bright sun;

under Granada's skies
there are deaths we'll always remember.

Things Seen in Spain

> Who has not seen Seville has not seen a marvel.
> *Spanish proverb*

> Give him alms, woman, for nothing in life can
> equal the agony of being blind in Granada.
> *Anon*

Death at five o'clock in the afternoon
A Cordobesque hack's hooves pummel the plain
A circus-ring hot with bullshit and blood
A hooded smile of irony and pain;
Unchaste virgins   immaculate matrons
Whoremasters sure their honour shows no stain
Life is a dream that dream-money can buy
And nobody's loss is nobody's gain;
Pinheaded angels thrust their dull points home
And yesterday's windmills are duly slain;
Today is already another day —
Tomorrow's the weakest link in the chain.
Each country gets the clichés it deserves:
— BRAVE BULL RAPES GYPSY DANCER IN OLD SPAIN —

Conquistador

> We came here to serve God, and also to get rich.
> *Bernal Díaz*

The poet
imposes
on the past
his uses.

Emperors
are clothed in
shirts and pin-
striped suits;

knights, unhorsed,
condemned for
slaying Moors
slaves, Negroes,

animals,
Indians…
— Pizarro
to monk who

spoke about
saving souls:
'I have not
come here for

such reasons.
I have come
to take from
them their gold.'

All art is
anachronism,
a quest
for riches

and treasures
never there,
a protest
that measures

which then were
impossible
to conceive
weren't taken.

Indignation
is not
historical;
those poets

who impose
their uses
on the past
abuse it.

Incident near Montserrat

He got back from market
and found the house empty.
She wasn't in the orchard
or the village café.

Alone in their kitchen
he felt the emptiness
but for an hour at least
pretended it wasn't there.

He grew hungry waiting
decided to start lunch
without her.
              Food and wine
tasted of her absence.
The radio voices
sounded off-key or blurred.
He couldn't find the breadknife.

Suddenly she is there
framed in the doorway
wearing only green tights
with his old crêpe bandage
wrapped strangely round her hands.

'...done something terrible,'
she mumbles.
              He jumps up
and runs to support her
but she flinches from him
as if she were unclean.

...She'd gone off to a wood
carrying the breadknife
and hacked at both her wrists...

She doesn't want a doctor.
She doesn't want him to see
her savaged wrists.
                        Gently
he inches her towards
the bathroom, bathes her wounds
redresses them, catches
her when she briefly faints.

Summoned by telephone
a neighbouring farmer
soon arrives to drive them
to the nearest clinic.

Three or four hours later
she's sitting up in bed
in a hospital ward
very white bandages
right up to her elbows.
The colour has come back
to her cheeks.
                        She has one
tendon slightly damaged.

Their troubled eyes exchange
looks of uncertainty.
'Do you want to leave me?'
He shakes his head slowly.
'I am full of remorse,'
she says.
        He kisses her
and smiles.
            He will bring her
cherries from the orchard
of their holiday home
not far from Montserrat.

Madrid: An Old Blind Woman

Led by a listless boy
Her hand on his shoulder
Her head thrown back
To counteract
Her stuttering steps,
She walks the hot streets
Of the city,
A smile on her lips
Her hair dyed blonde.

Craftsman

Cervantes, manco, escribe su gran novela con la mano que le falta.
A. Roa Bastos

(One-armed Cervantes writes his great novel with the hand he lacks.)

The trick is in the flick of the wrist
       the sound of one hand wringing
              a flight of fancy wings

That's what they want to hear: why not pretend it's true?
It would not do to risk or rock the market; so,
skill   style   signature   stamp of genius   and all
that counts as craft or gets called art becomes
an exercise in mutual flattery.

Prometheus was titanic
could afford to be a crank and not a crook.
The humble craftsman needs more cunning mentors;
Odysseus, for example, or his mate
Penelope, spinner of recycled yarn.

What they don't want to hear is fear as spur and rein
boring gestations   the birth-pangs of bias
or bitterness   amputation   prison   pain
the upbringing of offspring fated to be,
most of them, tax-collectors or sorely taxed.

I cut my losses when they severed my arm
       sent forth my knight armed only with illusions.

              And with a few tomfool tricks he deceived them all.

On Reading César Vallejo at Midnight

> I like life much less today
> but I always like living
> *César Vallejo*

I'm ill and on a diet,
the woman I love most (bad
dreams I had of her near dawn)
doesn't love me any longer,
I have no place of my own
to be sick in, make love in,
to order reference books
around the desk I write at.

And yet it has to be said
I sat under a blue sky,
ate my boiled fish with a friend,
talked about being unloved,
ill, alone, showed him photos
of my lost woman. Back home
in my borrowed room, I read
Vallejo, wrote a poem.

> I always like living but
> I liked living much less today;
> tomorrow's another day;
> today's almost yesterday.

Notes from Abroad

       I

At siesta time
in the public parks
of hot southern cities
there are always girls
scribbling letters home,
writing in notebooks
or secret journals.

      II

Her last visit here,
sixteen months ago,
she sat in this place
—an openair bar
by the boating lake—
took some photographs
and wrote her last poem.

Visit to a Dying Friend

   (for Pepe U.)

Outside the window
there's a spectacular sunset
half-lighting the Spanish landscape
but the man doesn't look
out of the window.

Time to say goodbye
For old friends who won't meet again
in Spain or England, but the man
who's lying there hasn't strength
to say goodbye

Doctor Esquerdo Street, Madrid

   In the morning
the sun lights up my desk;
   across the street
   they shiver;

   the evening sun
warms the terraces
   of my neighbours;
   I'm cold.

Welcome to Spain

They make everything
—absence, presence—
so easy, each cliché
comes with conviction
and reassuring
clap on the back.

All is superficial
yet meant and felt
dealt out at once
as novelty
and tribal wisdom
a folly to ignore.

Tomorrow they'll forget
once more, today
delight is genuine,
almost convincing
the traveller
he hasn't been away.

Picasso

...on ne parle pas au pilote.

You said: I don't seek, I find —
and so you did for more than
ninety years: women patrons
houses critics exegetes
hangers-on fellow-artists
and a hoard of found objects

You said: I make as I think
not as I see — and you made
blue beggars pink acrobats
distorted ladies snorting
minotaurs satyrs slow nymphs
deconstructed art-dealers

You wrote: Fire tongue fans her face —
throwing the words on the page
with the same diurnal rage
you used for drawing painting
sculpting ceramics etching
and for being Picasso

PATRIA (1990-2000)

The Bulls of Guisando or the Stillness of Stones

Nowhere near Guisando
and not at all like bulls
the bulls of Guisando
                       stand stoically
                       in an untidy field.
It's said their purpose was
to frighten marauding
tribes and cattle rustlers
                       at the same time serving
                       as boundary markers
but they seem so gentle
not a bit dangerous
the bulls of Guisando
                       keep one in your garden
                       they last three thousand years.

The ruins of Phaistos
the lions of Delos
the bulls of Guisando
                       homegrown Stonehenge
                                                   expose
                       the stillness of stones.

Spanish Character

He left it behind
to travel lighter
so it's his only
when he lands at Barajas,

when he smells warm air
blown from La Mancha
other tobacco
coffee noises exchanges

self-assured voices
and gestures talking
(which is forbidden)
to a talkative driver.

He puts on these things
without a mirror
and when we arrive
at the Colón terminal

in downtown Madrid
he's *madrileño*
again — alien
a foreigner but fitting.

Slaps on the shoulder:
Forty years—*hombre*—
you've known Spain longer
than most living Spaniards!

Revisiting Luarca: 1991

Your three-part palace,
bridged above the streets
by two galleries,
had lost its function:

One bit has become
the police station,
the other's being
converted into
a palace devoted
to art and culture,
the third–the chapel–
is now deserted.

(Years ago, on my
first visit there,
I proposed myself as
palace caretaker:
you chose to pretend
that I was joking.)

As I was leaving,
I found a hundred-
peseta coin
under the main arch:
I took it as your
legacy to me.

1492: Cowboys and Indians

(A contribution to the Columbus/Colón 5th centenary)

From an appropriately secured distance
(by which is meant: beyond the range of thrown spear
and sudden sally) we read the instrument
of abrupt and proper appropriation
whereby we award ourselves and successors
their–and their issue's–land liberty and limb...
And so on, and so forth, duly signed and sealed,
all parchment, goose quill, flourish and pink ribbon.

> And to make the symbolism
> clearer and stronger binding
> said instrument is written
> (and consequently proclaimed)
> in Castilian Spanish
> a language of which–as yet–
> they don't understand a word!
> Subtler than a serpent is
> the way of the Christians' God
> with whom we crucify them!

We laugh about this later in La Mancha
over rough red wine and even rougher cheese,
but for the next five hundred years it's fruitful
to believe in such self-serving sophistry.

Domenicos Theotocopoulos Becomes El Greco

How could a man, who first saw the light of day
on Crete and bathed in its blue waters,
settle for the barren landscape of Castile
with its thinly smiling spider king?

How exchange an island surrounded by sea
linked to Attica, Egypt, Venice,
for one encircled by arid desert, by
sterile protocol and bigotry?

And how survive there for nearly forty years
renamed with a nickname in a tongue
he never learned to master, and die there? –

By painting at the centre of an Empire
for a patron whose prime art was God
pictures that would outlive their passing sway.

Gredos: 1952

In the mountains of Spain
there were villages of old men
where you, on your hired mule,
became the first white man
(we use the two words imperially
as synonym for foreigner)
to reach them since before
the Civil War.

Yerma's Spain

Looking from my hotel window
at unwelcoming countryside
(In Spain, you can see the country
from the centre of a city),

I wondered why I found it hard
to compose a Spanish poem,
to spread the barren Spanish earth
over the fructifying page:

did one need Spanish words to coax
the coy Hispanic soul to yield
its wintery virginity
its summer crop of sun and shade?

or was it because, in Spain, all's
surface glitter, insubstantial
like the shimmer of sun and moon
on endless earth, on boundless sea?

or merely something to do with
geographical impatience,
some sort of topographical
incompetence, or a failure

(very common in translation)
to convey poesy and sense?

>   For poets
>   Picasso is a wall
>   on which to scribble
>   grafitti

Costa Brava: 1959

Old fishermen,
            bereft
                  of net and boat
their backs
         against the walls
                        of white houses,
sit in Catalan sun
            gazing at sea.

There was a young poet of Vigo
Who cast a cold eye towards Sligo:
    If it weren't for the Fates
    I might have been Yeats,
Thought this unsung young man from Vigo.

Comparative Literature

Because it is students not players who
Set the backdrop to its protagonist,
Alcalá de Henares seems much more
Accessible than Stratford-on-Avon;
Just as there are some who find Cervantes,
With his solitary knight and squire, more
Human than the polymorphous Shakespeare;
The former, too, is less hit by tourists
And the litter they shed like pigeon shit,
The smell of chips and shoddy souvenirs
Seem better kept at bay or out of sight.

Another fox and hedgehog case, another
Hare and tortoise race: Cervantes describes
Smaller circles; Shakespeare spills over into space.

Some Important Revelations about Picasso

> You knew him-I believe-this Picasso,
> studied him for a dozen years or so:
> what can you tell us about Picasso?

He had an Hispano and chauffeur to drive it,
a collection of paintings lodged in a bank vault
and plenty of real estate planted in France.
He spoke French with a strong Spanish accent,
he liked dressing up and wearing next to nothing,
he smoked like an old stove until one day he quit.
He kept pigeons, a goat, an Afghan hound
and a model series of colourful women.
When he died he was nearly ninety two years old.

> Thank you-have you anything more to add?

Yes, 'this Picasso' was a pretty good painter.

Charter Flight to Bilbao

The man, like himself, is wearing
    a basque beret,
his constant (mis)demeanour
    a mocking smile
as if to say: foreign travel
    is nothing new
merely a way of progressing
    to B from A.

His wife and knowing growing 'kids'
    swim in that smile,
basking, but wary, not wanting to drown.

Religious Sonnet

God died for me in Spain on Good Friday:

Burgos Nineteen Hundred and Fifty-One
At five o'clock in the afternoon, arms-
Reversed slow-marching soldiers in white gloves
Uniformed thin-moustached 'Movement' members
A General a Bishop civil guards
Priests, bare-footed penitents with scourges
Hidden citizens shuffling below floats
Bearing weeping Marys and bleeding Christs
(Petrified poses in polychromed wood) —
The arrogant terror of Church and State
Paraded to cow the spirit of Man.

On me it had an opposite effect:
Faint faith converted to firm unbelief.

Portuguesswork

There are plenty of portraits
of Fernando Pessoa:
slightly mysterious paintings
somewhat offguard photos drawings
as if caught in risqué comment
he had thought was inaudible;

but it has been impossible
to unearth images
of his alter egos:
Alberto Caeiro
Álvaro de Campos
or Ricardo Reis;

heteronymous poets
are seen only in print.

There was an Old Master called Pablo
Who produced a mass of Picassos
    'A sum of destructions'
    Which tempts the deduction
That life is less *vivant* than *tableaux*.

Chillida's *'Peine del Viento'* in San Sebastián

> Chillida's iron arcs
> rashly brave nature's tendency
> to rust man's works

For Antonio Machado

A far from avid reader of your verse
–And more at home with Don Abel Martín–
I find myself *metido* in your life
(The exact reverse of what should happen
But very much the fashion of this time.)

Though never planning to, I've tracked you down
First in Seville where you 'saw the light'
Then–leaving aside Madrid–Baeza
A scene of your teaching, next Soria
Where I walked your favoured walks, viewed your views,
And, yesterday, your Segovian house
(Most noted was a Picasso poster.)

I've even passed through Collioure where you died.

One day I'll read more closely what you wrote.

Goya's Disasters of War
Are no more than what he saw:
      It was his fate
      To illustrate
What wars are, not what they're for.

A Stab at Semantics

More than four's
a Spanish phrase
meaning many
or a lot,
maybe because
most mammals
have four legs —
but maybe not.

San Juan de Nieves: 1953

Each seaport has its harbour bore
who clasps you with his unforgetting claw
unable to grasp that
he who reminisces
misses the point about travel:
it must be a continuing measure,
passage, not from present to past,
but from bright past to dark future.

Castile: 1983

At Miranda maybe
I was drinking red wine
as we left the station.

Outside the *Cantina*
A man on the platform
was also drinking wine.

Almost together, we
raised glasses in salute,
then, immediately
my train left him behind.

The Distance of Spain

> Lejana y sola
> *F. García Lorca*

In Spain
even today
fifty years later
you can still glimpse
distance.

Shadows
fleeting across
her barren landscapes
seem to highlight
distance.

Those days
through slow moving
train windows you saw
made palpable
distance.

These days
from her swarming
motorways you get
quick snatches of
distance.

For Spain
-aloof, alone,
remote-manages
still to keep her
distance.

Patria

In those days of exile
I rarely thought of home —
'Ex-home' I should have said.

Now I am home again
Remembering 'abroad'
And waiting to be dead.

For a complete list of Hearing Eye publications, please write enclosing an SAE to:

Hearing Eye,
Box 1,
99 Torriano Avenue,
London
NW5 2RX

Alternatively, please visit the Hearing Eye website at:

http://www.torriano.org